Dandelion Princess

written by

Sandra Rippetoe

illustrated by

Joan Zehnder

Nature's
Rhyme
Harrodsburg, KY

The text type was set in Comic Sans MS

Library of Congress Control Number: 2021952506
ISBN: 979-8-9854114-0-9 (paperback)
ISBN: 979-8-9854114-1-6 (ebook)

Printed in the United States of America

With sincere gratitude to
Ed Rippetoe and Olivia Rippetoe for the
lovely photograph that inspired the story,
"Dandelion Princess"

In Forest-So-Green
near a wintertime meadow . . .

lived a dandelion princess
who in March showed her shadow.

She'd most likely appear
in a morn's misty dew –
mysterious was she
and magical too.

A creative spirit
and keeper of the land,

she could heal the earth
with the touch of her hand.

They decided to talk
  to the seed guarding gnome.
He was her friend.
  They set off for his home . . .

calling out his name
  since he couldn't be seen
under the tree roots
  in Forest-So-Green.

"I have not spied her.
    This year is so strange,"
explained the small gnome.
    "It's a worrisome change.
But it's my opinion
    perhaps she is hiding.
She goes by the rules . . .
    laws of nature abiding.
. Let's hope, by April,
    she then will come out.
Without her our lives
    would be altered, no doubt!"

April came and went with no dandelion princess.

On the 1st day of May things looked grim, I confess.

But then on May 2nd
   in the late afternoon,
she arrived at long last
   not a minute too soon.

The fields and the forests
   became dotted with yellow.
The bees came thereafter.
   Winter left with no bellow.

It was such a relief
    to see everything green.
And the dandelion princess?
    A most beautiful scene!

Because when she arrived,
    then springtime could start.
The world came to life,
    and hope filled each heart!

Sandra Rippetoe, MA, RDN, LD is a poet, author, registered dietitian nutritionist, and former homeschool teacher. Sandra loves spending time outdoors in nature. She's especially fond of dandelions and bees! She's the author of another children's book, *The Perceptive Peonies*. Sandra lives in Kentucky with her husband and son. Please visit her online at naturesrhyme.com.

Joan Zehnder, MFA is an artist, author, teacher, and retired art therapist. Even as a child, Joan saw herself as an artist and spent many hours creating with crayons, watercolors, and pencils. She is the author of three books of paintings: *Imaginings*, *Threshold*, and *Creative Energy*, and the illustrator of another children's book, *The Perceptive Peonies*. For more information on Joan's art, please visit saatchiart.com/joanzehnder.